Tiger toast to Jungle jam

a rainforest alphabet

written & illustrated by Sandra Mohr

Tiger Toast to Jungle Jam
A Rainforest Alphabet

© 2010 Sandra Mohr

All rights reserved. No part of this book may be reproduced by any means, whether electronic or otherwise, except for brief excerpts which may be used by reviewers.

Published by:
Winters Publishing
P.O. Box 501
Greensburg, IN 47240
winterspublishing.com
812-663-4948

ISBN 10: 1-883651-41-7
ISBN 13: 978-1-883651-41-1

Library of Congress Control Number: 2010932289

Printed in the United States of America

For: Karina

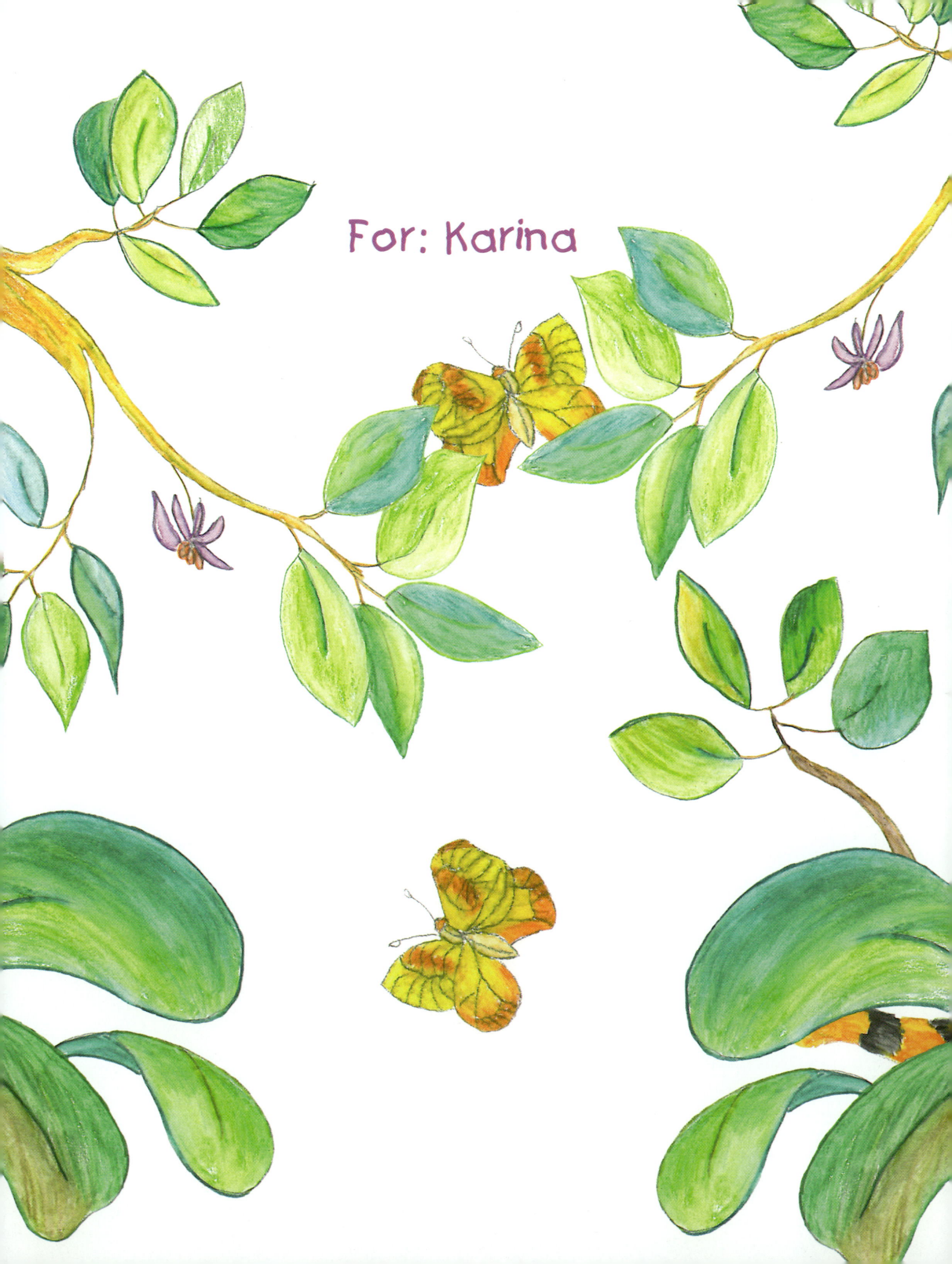

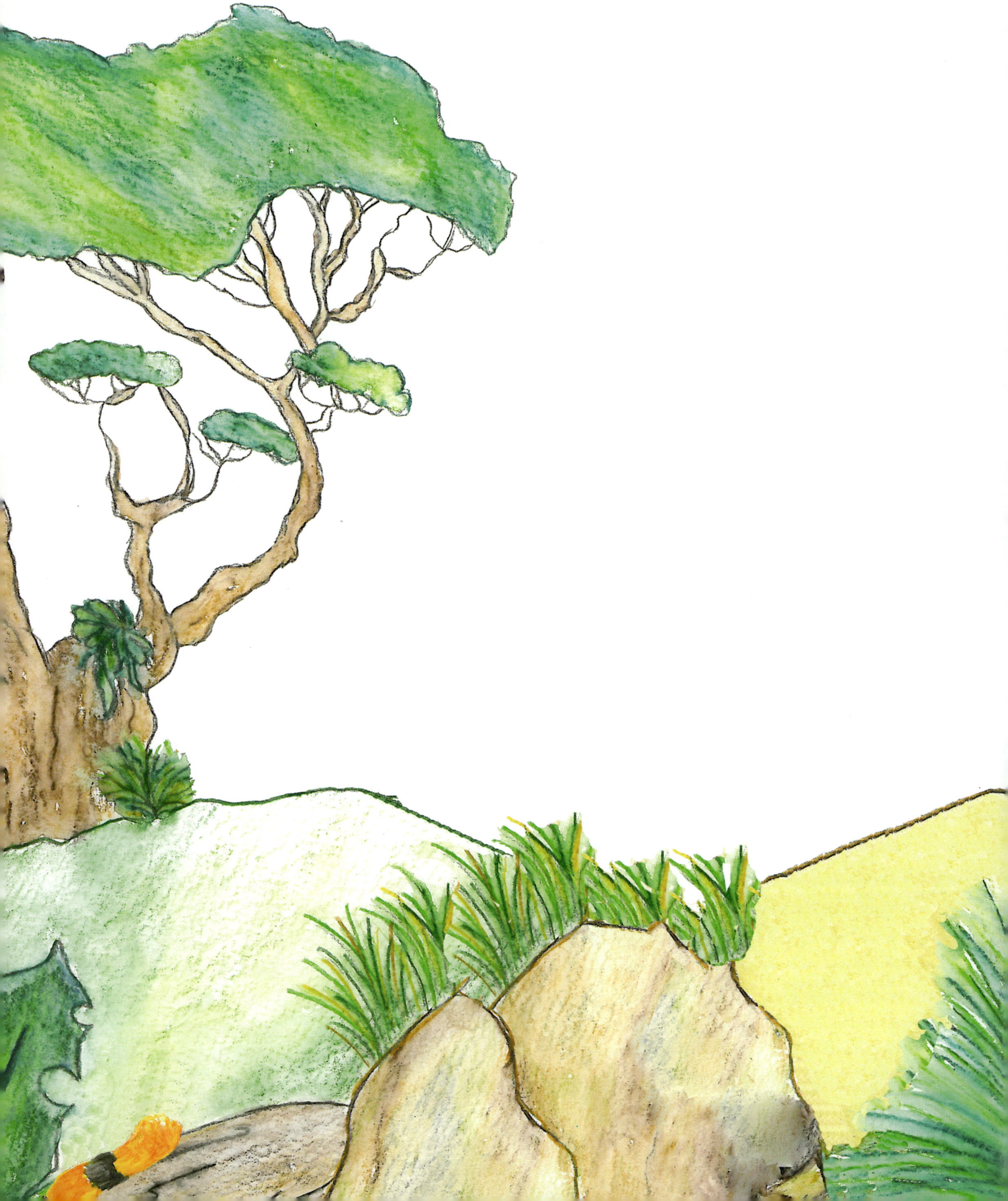

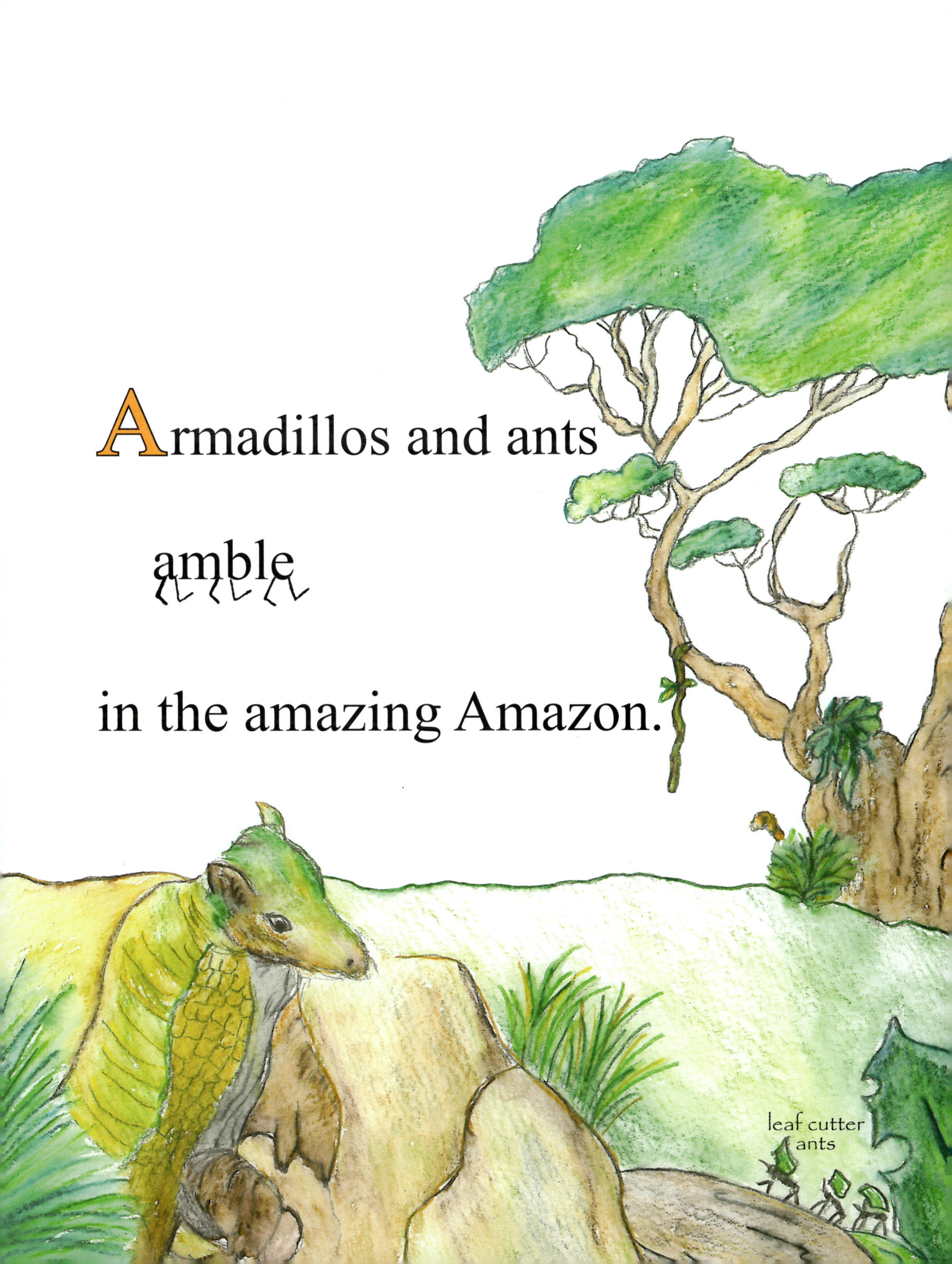

Armadillos and ants amble in the amazing Amazon.

leaf cutter ants

Beautiful

butterflies

boogie

from

branch

to branch.

glasswing butterfly
mimosa butterfly
yolk butterfly
morpho butterfly

Chameleons change colors under the canopy's curtain.

Dragonflies drone

as the

dwarf mongoose

dreams.

Elegant elephants eat from elongated trunks.

Fanciful frogs flip flip and flit on the forest floor.

glass frog
red-eyed frog
gladiator frog
poison-dart frog

Golden eyes gleam from the great horned owl.

Hummingbirds

hover

in the

humid

air.

Iguanas idle in iridescent splendor.

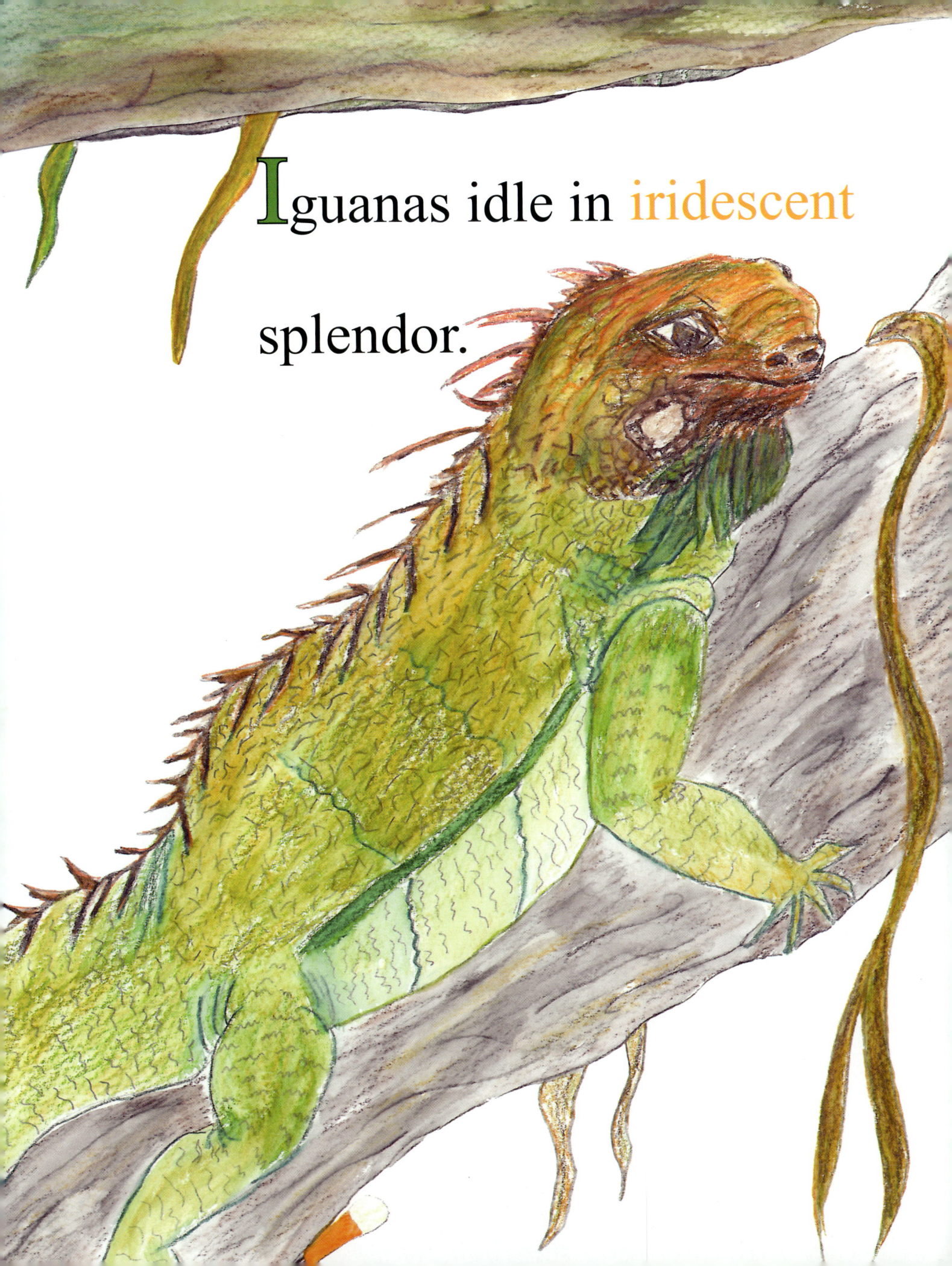

Jaguars jump to the jungle jam.

Kinkajous

are keen

to keep

to themselves.

Lazily,

lemurs loll upon

lush

limbs.

Marmosets and monkeys mingle and mix.

gibbon

marmoset

Neon Tetras nibble

and

navigate narrow waters.

Orangutans observe us observing them.

Pretty, powerful

or

petite,

parakeet

their parts

are perfectly

played.

Philippine eagle

collared puffbird

Peperomia vine

Quetzal's
colorful quills quietly quiver in the Calabash trees.

Raccoons

roam

in the

refreshing rain.

eyelash viper

S...s...sassy snakes

swing

green anaconda

king cobra

in the sizzling sun.

Tigers toast

in the tropical

trees.

Unique

uakaris

are

unmistakable

in the

undergrowth.

Velvety voles visit vast valleys in search of vittles.

Wide-eyed western tarsiers

watch the world.

Xenosaurs are excitable when it's extremely dark.

Yellow (rumped) cacique's flute-like yells

yield

good

news.

Zebra-wings zip a

zany

zig-

zag

through   the sky.

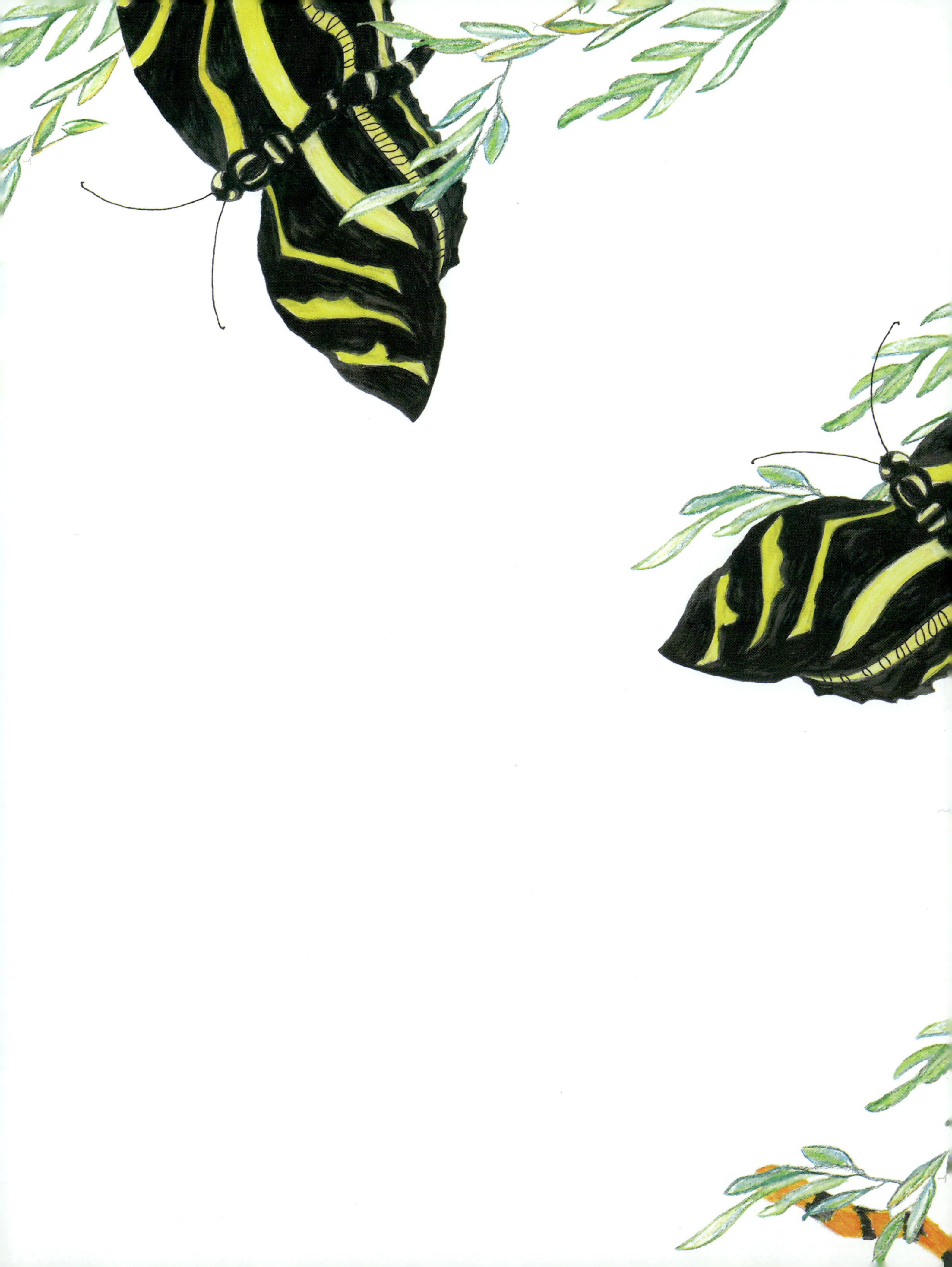

About The Author

Sandra Mohr is also the author of *March To The Sea*, a picture book on sea turtles and conservation. Born in Michigan, with Ponce Inlet, Florida as a second home in her heart, she loves to bring the beauty and mystery of nature to her readers. Bright illustrations in watercolor pencil add life to her words. She currently lives in Indiana with her husband and daughter.